ARMED
PATRIOTS

By

Will Clark

ARMED PATRIOTS

Copyright© 2015 by Will Clark

ISBN-13: 978-1511576864
ISBN-10: 1511576863

Published by
Motivation Basics
P.O. Box 6327
Diamondhead, MS 39525
Will01@aol.com

QUOTE

"A nation can survive its fools, and even the ambitious. But it cannot survive treason from within. An enemy at the gates is less formidable, for he is known and carries his banner openly. But the traitor moves amongst those within the gate freely, his sly whispers rustling through all the alleys, heard in the very halls of government itself. For the traitor appears not a traitor; he speaks in accents familiar to his victims, and he wears their face and their arguments, he appeals to the baseness that lies deep in the hearts of all men. He rots the soul of a nation, he works secretly and unknown in the night to undermine the pillars of the city, he infects the body politic so that it can no longer resist. A murderer is less to fear. The traitor is the plague."
Marcus Tullius Cicero, 58 B.C. Speech in the Roman Senate

SNAKES

Would you stroll barefoot through snake-infested grass?

Only if you want those snakes to kill you.

Would you wait for an enemy to attack you before you
consider owning a weapon?

Only if you want that snake to kill you.

There are two kinds of snakes:

Snakes in the grass don't strike unless you disturb them.

That other snake seeks you out to destroy you;
He was first discovered in the Garden of Eden;
His name is Evil.

HE VOWS TO KILL YOU.
YOU MUST BE ARMED
AND
PREPARED TO DEFEAT HIM.

CONTENTS

Article 1

The Second Amendment

In the Bill of Rights, the Second Amendment to the Constitution reads:

"A well regulated Militia, being necessary to the security of a free State, the right of the people to keep and bear Arms shall not be infringed."

The real purpose and intent of the wording of this amendment has been argued for decades. Historically, it has meant two different things to people depending upon their opinions and preferences regarding gun control. Even members of our Supreme Court differ on the interpretation, ordinarily based on their political leanings and preferences; and to whom they owe allegiance for their appointments.

Those justices appointed by a Democrat president who prefers strict gun control ordinarily hold to that conviction with their votes. Justices appointed by Republican presidents ordinarily vote the opposite view; that the freedom to keep and bear arms is an individual right.

All historical documents that explain the purpose for the Second Amendment, the right to keep and bear arms, reference the primary purpose for that amendment; to maintain the means to repel a tyrannical federal government that might take away those liberties guaranteed by our Constitution. The original writers expressed the idea that man's natural leaning is to instinctively grasp more personal power for himself; and given that position as president might not refuse himself from doing so if given any leeway to take that action. As commander-in-chief, a president would have that inherent power, authority, and position. It was assumed, at that time, that any foreign invader would be repelled by the standing national army.

Wording, intentions, perspectives and time sway interpretations of those few words in the Second Amendment. For example, the word 'Militia' was written, and considered, at a time when individual states were considered more independent from the federal government. Since that time, the name has changed from 'Militia' to 'National Guard.' Even the new title 'National' suggests or implies that these state units no longer exist just for the protection of a state, as in a 'State Militia.' When necessary, or when expedient for a national purpose, the commander-in-chief can activate them - and they are no longer a 'state militia.'

In effect; a state militia, now a National Guard Unit, is no longer free to maintain a state free from the military encroachment of a federal military unit - they are part of that federal military unit. This simple understanding circumvents the intended purpose for the words written at that time - the time of the Second Amendment's creation. To maintain the purpose for the words of the Second Amendment, the other words must be considered. They are:

"...the right of the people to keep and bear Arms shall not be infringed."

If we understand the purpose of the Second Amendment to be the protection of states, and of the people of those states, then the people's protection must be paramount. States no longer have a Constitutional right to protect themselves - they are now part of the whole, militarily. Clearly, our Founding Fathers understood the weaknesses and vulnerability of those given power to seek more and greater power even at the expense of individual freedom of the nation's citizens. Obviously, they realized a fully armed citizenry was urgent to maintain reasonable actions from what could be a less than benign leader; one who might be guided to tyranny by a power lust.

Considering words, time, and separation of power, only one conclusion can reasonably be made about the interpretation of those few words. Each competent and responsible American citizen has the right to own a weapon, and for two purposes:

First is to fulfill the tenets of the Second Amendment. That is to discourage tyranny from power-lust leaders who have the power and position to fulfill that lust.

Second is to fulfill our God-given right to protect ourselves and our families against any evil-doer who would threaten our existence. God put us here; certainly He meant for no earthly person to take that life from us. A gun is a weapon of defense that helps us feel secure in this land of individual freedom - at least freedom as we exist at this moment in time.

There is also a Bible verse that discusses the concept of security as a means of deception. Daniel 8:25 says: "He will cause deceit to prosper, and he will consider himself superior. *When they feel secure,* he will destroy many and take his stand against the Prince of princes." What could this concept of security mean to us in our present time, and as paralleled in the Bible? It means that perhaps the emphasis on 'security' will be the tool to take our weapons from us.

Could this possibly mean that when Barack Obama, or any other president in the future, confiscates our weapons, it will be under the pretense of making us more 'secure?' The guise might well be that if no one owns a weapon everybody will be secure and safe. This is the claim of those who now so strongly support more gun control. It's their powerful mantra. It's the only argument they can propose. Their argument has Biblical implications.

If that were to happen; if powerful leaders were to confiscate our guns, our defenses, could that in any way make us safer? Absolutely not. It would mean our government would have no hesitancies to further encroach upon our Constitutional rights, and we would be vulnerable to personal attacks by anyone who would have a weapon; we would be totally defenseless. That means if anyone wants to kill or otherwise injure us, we would be helpless and defenseless - not safe and secure. But how could this confiscation happen? It could happen in the name of 'safety' and 'security.'

All it would take is one simple terrorist attack in America. All it would take is for a president to declare martial law because we 'are under threat from terrorism' and it will make everything 'safer' if no one has a weapon. If that were to happen, only the government and the terrorists would have weapons. That would be our death sign. It would be the death of America as we know it.

To create and allow our highest possibility of safety in America, not only should every competent and responsible citizen in America be allowed to own weapons; every citizen should be required to own a weapon. Furthermore, they should be taught how to use those weapons effectively to defend our nation and our freedom. Everyone working together, including our federal government; that's the real meaning of America: freedom and liberty.

Why would anyone suggest otherwise; that patriotic and competent citizens should not be allowed to own personal firearms? That question has only one of two answers. Either that person does not understand our Constitution and the Second Amendment; or that person hates our Constitution and all it stands for: personal freedom and liberty.

Who in our lifetime has expressed such disdain and hatred toward our Constitution and the other freedom writings our Founding Fathers gave us? Only one person fits that description, and it's our current president, Barack Hussein Obama. His hatred of our Constitution will be discussed next.

Article 2

Constitutional Protections

We have had many presidents throughout the history of our great nation, the United States of America. Some have been better than others in accomplishing appointed and expected goals and duties, and some have not been so effective. Regardless of their effectiveness and mission accomplishment they all had one common positive trait. All their actions and words never left any doubt they loved their country, and would fulfill their mission to the best of their ability; and in compliance with the established goals of our Constitution. Until our current president, Barack Obama, not a single one ever showed such disdain against the Constitution or our Founding Fathers who wrote those freedoms for us. Barack Obama is the exception. He has openly expressed his hatred of our Constitution. He has also criticized those who designed and planned our freedoms.

During a September 2001 Chicago public radio program Barack Obama said the U.S. Constitution was flawed and even stressed it had "deep flaws." He then accused those Founding Fathers who wrote our Constitution of having "an enormous blind spot" when they wrote it. In his radio talk, he said the fundamental flaw it reflected about this country continues even today. At that time he didn't go into enough details to explain what he meant. Later discussions and disclosures indicated, however, that he believed more of the Constitution should have been written to insure more equitable distribution of wealth - which has been confirmed by his later words, actions, and policies.

When this radio conversation was revealed in 2008, many questioned how he could effectively and sincerely take the oath of office. Rush Limbaugh even said, "Good Lord, ladies and gentlemen! I don't see how he can take the oath of office, which is this: 'I do solemnly swear, or affirm, that I will faithfully execute the office of President of the United States, and I will to the best of my ability preserve, protect, and defend the Constitution of the United States." Limbaugh added, "He has rejected the Constitution."

Perhaps Obama's intention to show his disdain for the Constitution was further demonstrated when he made other statements in 2001 as reported by inforwars.com on June 12, 2013. Their article is titled: Obama Calls Constitution 'Charter of Negative Liberties.'

In that radio interview he said, "The Constitution was a charter of negative liberties, full of constraints imposed upon us by our Founding Fathers." Later Obama reportedly also said, in response to the situation with Edward Snowden's revelation regarding wiretaps and exposure of other monitoring of individual citizens, "You can't have 100-percent security and also have 100-percent privacy and zero inconvenience. We're going to have to make some choices as a society." In 2013, a Pew Research Poll showed that 56 percent of Americans agreed with him - that security was too important not to take more drastic measures for safety.

Obama made other extreme statement in 2001, including this one, "The Supreme Court never ventured into the issues of redistribution of wealth, and of more basic issues such as political and economic justice in society." He continued, saying the Supreme Court didn't break free from the essential constraints that were placed by the Founding Fathers in the Constitution, at least as it's been interpreted. He also stated that the Warren Court interpreted the Constitution as a charter of "negative liberties." Obama emphasized that the Constitution says what the states and the federal government can't do to you; but not what they must do on your behalf.

What does all this mean, and why does Barack Obama so strongly oppose it: a Constitution that allows and grants us as individual citizens, liberty and freedom; especially from oppression and suppression by the federal government? The clue to the answer comes from his very words, "The Supreme Court never ventured into the issues of redistribution of wealth, and of more basic issues such as political and economic justice in society." Do you realize what these words mean; the seriousness they suggest; the challenge to our freedoms they insinuate? These words and the ideas suggest our rights of life, liberty, and the pursuit of happiness come from government and not from God. These words, not thoughts, suggest tyranny against those things forming the bedrock of our lives and aspirations; our U.S. Constitution. In effect, he hates, he disdains, he criticizes the very bedrock and foundation that establishes our liberty and rights to success and happiness.

Much earlier when Obama burst upon the political scene he often used the terms 'Social Justice' and 'Economic Justice.' Perhaps realizing the base of these terms and the ideologies they represented, he changed his rhetoric to other terms such as: fair share, equitable distribution, equity, a fair chance, and redistributive justice. Recently, he used the term 'social justice' again. Perhaps he thought it wouldn't be noticed in the forum at that time. A post by Juliet Eilperin from the washingtonpost.com, on October 10, 2014, reported:

"SAN DIMAS -- Standing under hot and hazy skies with the San Gabriel Mountains behind him, President Obama set aside 346,000 acres of U.S. forestland as a national monument Friday.

Calling it "an issue of social justice," Obama said that "for a lot of urban families, this is their only big outdoor space."

Obviously, he can't totally eliminate that thought of 'social justice' from his psyche. This idea or this concept is more important that one considering it only casually might suspect. The concept of 'Social Justice' is the foundation of all the Socialist and Communist movements throughout history. A study of his background reveals Obama patterned much of his ideology after one whose principles he read, studied and taught; Saul Alinsky.

Saul Alinsky wrote as one of his principles of radicalism, "Mankind has been and is divided into three parts: the Haves, the Have-Nots, and the Have-a-Little, Want Mores." This division of economic society forms the basis for radicalism and other 'isms' that tends to destroy a working and homogeneous society.

Alinsky's principle shown above, is the clearest signal that he patterned his design for radical change after the success in Russia of Marx, Ingals, and Lenin in their 'Rise of the Proletariat.' George Orwell described these three levels in his book '1984.' In his book, Orwell described the Have-Nots as the Proles, as Russia had designated the 'working class' as the Proletariat. Accordingly, this is the normal pattern to incite the working class to rise from frustration and desperation, and have hope for a better life - not even understanding what that better life might be; thus making them Useful Idiots. Obama clearly recognizes this principle as he forms, molds, and leads his followers with nose-rings to promised riches and happiness.

18

As Lenin categorized them, they turn themselves into 'Useful Idiots' as they follow Obama into his promised world of prosperous bliss. There's only one major problem they don't recognize, because they never stop to look and ask. They never find that promised land. As Orwell explained in his book, they are used until the 'middle' achieve their goals to replace the 'high,' then they are cast back down to the 'low.' They are never advanced; they never, never reach that promised land. Not only do they never reach it, they are never able even to describe that land in which they hope to arrive. They simply flounder in a void totally obscured by thick fog. They continue to seal their lost destiny themselves by refusing to wear shoes in snake-infested grass.

So what happened in Russia after Lenin accomplished his social revolution by using the proletariat, the working class, to overthrow the existing government? Czar Nicolas and his family were murdered and all national leaders were killed or exiled. Did the working class, described by Orwell as the 'Lows' advance themselves either economically or socially by following the one who promised them economic and social advancement? Surprise! Their life became worse and more miserable.

The Communist movement in Russia, largely by Vladimir Lenin and Joseph Stalin, resulted in poverty, despair, and the slaughter of millions of citizens - many of whom had been the strongest supporters of the orchestrated movement. Anyone who expressed discontent with the system was annihilated - or sent to Siberia to die a harsh death. Many of Stalin's greatest supporters were oblivious to the fact that he was the one who ordered their deaths and their banishment. They supported him until their last breath believing that 'Uncle Joe' was their friend and supporter.

But, Russia is not unique. Every other country converting to

Socialism or Communism has experienced the same results. Millions of people are killed in the transition, individuality is taken from those citizens, and despair becomes the normal aspiration of the average citizen. Socialism destroys individual hope and aspirations except for those few, the 'High' who remain in control.

This leads one to ask why Barack Obama is so intent to enforce his ideologies of 'sharing the wealth' and implementing more 'social justice.' These concepts, when implemented, always result in despair and destitution, and most often into tyranny and subjugation. His economic and social leanings help explain his hatred of our U.S. Constitution. That Constitution is there to shield us and to protect us from tyranny and harm. What are his plans? Why doesn't he respect our Constitution? He seems to be leading us toward Socialism or Communism.

But, wait! Perhaps that's only a distraction toward something more insidious and evil. What are his real plans, and how does it affect our safety and security? Before we discuss that alternative, let's first take a good look at his obvious trend - disruption and Socialism as proposed by Saul Alinsky.

Article 3

Destroying the Status Quo

It appears Obama's natural tendency is to lead us down the road to Socialism. He was trained by bona fide Socialists; he had family members who are/were Socialists; and his rhetoric about 'sharing the wealth' etc. is all about Socialism. It appears that's where he wants to take us - to move the United States away from the freedoms offered under our Constitution and our free enterprise economic system. 'Share' and 'Redistribution' are the mantras of Socialists that began with Marx and Ingles; and all who followed them. These two words sound harmless and Christianly, but regarding the future of a nation, nothing could be further from the truth. They form a dangerous rally cry for those determined to destroy a nation.

Obama's immediate family members were Socialists; and in his younger years while living in Hawaii, his grandfather even introduced him to a card-carrying Communist named Frank Marshall Davis. His grandfather chose Davis to be Obama's mentor specifically because Davis was a Socialist-Communist.

When Obama became president he immediately surrounded himself with Communists, or those who had Communist leanings or associations. These included Valerie Jarrett and David Axelrod. Two other close Communist associates included Van Jones and Anita Dunn. Van Jones became so blatantly radical that he was finally forced out from Obama's circle by too much public pressure.

Anita Dunn finally had to resign her post when a backlash was created from a statement she made on October 16, 2009. In that statement she said that Mao Tse-Tung was one of her favorite philosophers, and the one that she, "turns to the most." Mao was the Communist leader that starved, tortured, and murdered 70 million Chinese when he took over China.

Obama quickly surrounded and nurtured himself with fellow Communists/Socialists when he became president of the United States. He also immediately began assimilating all those important words and concepts announcing his disdain for our Constitution and his leaning toward destroying the protections offered beneath that banner. Not only had he been introduced to those concepts he also taught those radical concepts before he became president; while he was a 'community organizer.' In his role as a community organizer, he was trained in and taught the concepts of Saul Alinsky, as outlined in Alinksy's two books.

Alinsky's two important books are: 'Rules for Radicals' and 'Reveille for Radicals.' In the books he details and describes the process in creating a different state; to destroy the status quo. He gives eight levels of control before a social state can be created. The first is the most important.

1) Healthcare– 'Control healthcare and you control the people.'

This was Obama's first and most critical action when he became president. He didn't hesitate; he immediately began his healthcare project as soon as he became president. Fortunately for him, he had just enough Democrats in the Senate to pass his bill for health care. Not one single Republican senator voted for it. Even worse, during his campaign for his health care program he was deceptive and deceitful. His deceptions were so powerful they conjured up visions of the Deceiver introduced in the Bible Book of Genesis, and further described in the Books of Daniel and Revelation. His falsehoods were so great that the question of any honesty from his lips must seriously be considered.

2) Poverty – 'Increase the poverty level as high as possible, poor people are easier to control and will not fight back if you are providing everything for them to live.'

Just look how Obama has created a broader welfare state; welfare, food stamps, special programs to distribute the wealth. His actions have also eliminated many good jobs that existed before he became president. His administration even established units to promote and distribute more food stamps to Americans - obviously to make them feel poorer and more helpless. The more Obama can convince citizens not to, as the Bible says, "earn their own bread," the more uninspired followers he can create. (2 Thessalonians 3:12)

Since he has been president, the average earned income has decreased by $2000. Yes, Barack Obama understands that to accomplish his goals he must create more poverty. Also, there's little doubt that the primary purpose for his unending zeal to bring millions of illegal immigrants into our country is to expand this poverty pool. His other purpose clearly is to create a larger pool of 'useful innocents' to continue voting for his policies to destroy America's foundation based on liberty and opportunity. He wants to give future Americans what he considers their 'fair share.' Of course, that's a fair share of the left-over bread crumbs after he destroys what he describes as the 'millionaires and billionaires.'.

3) Debt – 'Increase the debt to an unsustainable level. That way

you are able to increase taxes, and this will produce more poverty.'

Obama has increased the national debt faster and greater than any president ever. It's now over 18 trillion dollars - and growing. He doesn't even discuss the national debt or what to do about it. He occasionally mentions 'budget deficit' which is not the same as the national debt. His favorite tactic is to hold Congress hostage by including necessary spending, such as national defense and border security with other spending bills. That way he can blame Congress for not caring about the defense of our nation. It's a simple and obvious tactic, but it works to convince his minions and other useful innocents that he's the only one concerned about our safety.

4) Gun Control– 'Remove the ability to defend themselves from the government. That way you are able to create a police state.'

Obama hasn't taken drastic actions to create gun control - but he often approaches the subject. If he gains more power, certainly this will be his first action - in the name of 'security.' While Islamic terrorists are attacking and terrorizing all over the world, he continues to nip away at the edges of gun control trying to find a vulnerable space to pry guns and ammunition from the hands of patriotic Americans.

As only one current example, this is an article submitted by Michael F. Haverluck at OneNewsNow.com on February 20, 2015. This article explains the latest attempt by the Obama administration to chip away at gun rights. The article is titled, 'NRA, others: Obama not done with unilateral moves on gun control':

"The aggressiveness of the Obama administration in its war on guns already this year has surprised even the National Rifle

Association.

A Closer Look: Unloading his latest round of gun-control legislation, President Barack Obama's executive fiat is poised to stop Americans from buying and selling a traditional form of ammunition that has been one of the country's favorites for generations — the .223-caliber "green-tipped" bullet. It's commonly used in an array of rifles sold at local sporting goods store.

The "justification" behind the Obama administration's ban is based on the availability of a new kind of revolver that can use the same ammunition made for general-purpose rifles. Some gun-control advocates — including those staffed at the White House — flag this ammo as "armor-piercing," according to WND's Leo Hohmann.

News of the White House's move to try and further squelch the freedoms of gun-toting Americans — by keeping them from loading their favorite "green-tipped" rounds — had an immediate effect on Valentine's Day.

"The Bureau of Alcohol, Tobacco, Firearms and Explosives (BATFE) announced on February 14 a proposed ban on the manufacture, sale or importation of a popular form of ammunition used by thousands of law-abiding gun owners," reports Hohmann. "Within hours of the announcement, the prices on the green-tipped .223-caliber rounds started skyrocketing."

Restricting munitions for rifle owners was not the intent behind the Gun Control Act of 1968 that Congress amended in 1986 to keep criminals with handguns from accessing the "cop killer" bullets from store shelves. It was already known and accepted that an AR-15 or any other high-powered hunting rifle firing the bullet could pierce a police officer's soft body armor.

"This is just another example of the Obama administration using executive authority to attack the rights of gun owners," Second Amendment Foundation founder and executive vice president Alan Gottlieb contended, reports WND. "Obama thinks he is 'dictator in chief' and can go around Congress to ban ammunition and punish legitimate gun owners. The Obama administration has doubled down on their war on gun owners."

Gottlieb isn't the only gun-rights advocate who is appalled at Obama's latest attempt to steamroll American's right to bear arms — with accessible bullets, that is.

Same route, different agenda:

GeorgiaCarry.org executive director Jerry Henry insists that the president's appeal to executive action to force his latest highly contended campaign against gun owners is reminiscent of his dictatorial handling of the unilateral action he took to push amnesty through for illegal immigrants.

.233 green-tipped ammo 620x300: "This move is nothing less than this administration taking the law into their own hands, bypassing Congress and their constitutional duties of writing and passing legislation," Henry decried to WND. "This administration has failed to pass gun-control legislation through the constitutional process. They have failed at the polls to pass meaningful gun control, and they have failed to win in the courts,"

Henry attests this latest effort by the White House is merely the president's last-ditch attempt to advance his gun-control agenda at any cost.

"The only way left is through illegal processes and backdoor regulations," Henry continued. "The American people have spoken to the gun-control antics of this administration, but this administration refuses to listen."

Henry told WND that the current administration has reversed the "master and servant" relationship that American citizens were intended to have with government and its officials. He says the federal powers have now grabbed the reins and continue to straight-arm Americans, ordering them what to do — not only without their blessing, but against their will.

"If this is not stopped and stopped now, this administration will continue to push their agenda to disarm the American citizens with the goal of making them slaves to the U.S. government," Henry alerted WND. "Citizens have the right to be armed. Slaves to the U.S. government will have no such right."

Chipping away at citizen's rights:

According to Henry, Obama is masterfully putting the process of incremental-ism into action, building upon Congress' Gun Control Act of the '60s and Reagan's "armor-piercing" ban of the '80s only to eradicate one of its major exceptions.

"If he gets by with this, I believe he will not stop in his efforts to disarm us via regulations," Henry stressed.

The National Rifle Association (NRA) states the M855 ball bullet has absolutely no business being classified as "armor-piercing" ammunition because it is "primarily intended for sporting purposes." Furthermore, it argues that because the bullet has a traditional lead core — not steel, bronze, brass, beryllium copper, depleted uranium or beryllium copper, as all armor-piercing bullets do — it cannot be legitimately classified as "armor-piercing."

The aggressiveness of the Obama administration this year in its war on guns has even surprised the NRA, which has been battling with the White House over its gun-control agenda since the president took office more than six years ago.

"It isn't even the third week of February, and the BATFE has already taken three major executive actions on gun control," the NRA announced. "First, it was a major change to what activities constitute regulated 'manufacturing' of firearms. Next, BATFE reversed a less-than-year-old position on firing a shouldered 'pistol.' Now, BATFE has released a 'Framework for Determining Whether Certain Projectiles Are Primarily Intended for Sporting Purposes Within the Meaning of 18 U.S.C. 921(a)(17)(c),' which would eliminate M855's exemption to the armor-piercing ammunition prohibition and make future exemptions nearly impossible."

Pointing out that it's just a matter of time before Obama bypasses Congress again to assert his extreme gun-control agenda, Gottlieb is certain that round two is already in the works.

"Obama will use his executive powers to do as much damage as he can get away with," Gottlieb warns. "This is not the end of his attack on Second Amendment rights." End of article.

5) Welfare – 'Take control of every aspect of their lives.'

This was described earlier under health care and poverty. It includes food, housing, income and other freebies such as personal cell phones. It's the ultimate 'Big Brother' scenario.

6) Education – 'Take control of what people read and listen to – take control of what children learn in school.'

Common core and Obama's new proposals for free 2-year college education are current examples of his effort to control this arena.

7) Religion – 'Remove the belief in the God from the Government and schools.'

Obama and his minions have already accomplished this. And, in too many cases they have replaced Christianity with Islam in many public places. Obama welcomes many Islamic leaders into the White House without offering that same openness to Christian leaders. His many other anti-Christian and anti-God actions are easily accessible on the internet. I have described at least five other blatant atrocities against Christianity by Obama in my previous books.

8) Class Warfare – 'Divide the people into the wealthy and the poor. This will cause more discontent and it will be easier to take (Tax) the wealthy with the support of the poor.'

Does anyone doubt that he has not already further separated the rich and the poor in our country? He never fails to promote the idea that the poor are poor because the rich have taken so much from them. What other reason would he continue to promote that idea other than to make the poor people hate the rich people? There could be no other conceivable reason than to divide the people.

Alinsky merely simplified Vladimir Lenin's original scheme for world conquest by communism, under Russian rule. Stalin described his converts as "Useful Idiots." The Useful Idiots have destroyed every nation in which they have seized power and control. It is presently happening at an alarming rate in the U.S. According to Alinsky: "It is difficult to free fools from the chains they revere."

In summary, America - 'we' - are being attacked on three fronts. First is the direct Islamic terrorist attacks. Second is the Islamists' plan to take over America by subterfuge and stealth. Third is the movement by highly influential people to transition America into a socialist country instead of a free country. Or, according to Alinsky's plan, just to destroy the status quo, of who we are without anything better to replace that status quo.

What can we do to resist these attacks? First, understand these three separate and distinct dangers. Inform others; and when election time comes, vote for a candidate who loves America as it was conceived by our Founding Fathers who created our Constitution to guide our nation into prosperity and a long history of freedom. Our freedom is being undermined by those who deceitfully promise great things to those who are vulnerable to accept those deceptions.

The purpose for this book, however, is to urge every patriotic American citizen to arm himself or herself. We must be armed to demonstrate to any terrorist who would attack us, individually or as a large group, that we are Americans and we will not tolerate it. They should know without any doubt that we fully intend to personally, and as a nation, defend our great nation - even if that means putting a bullet through their evil heads. Without bullets and guns, our nation would never have been born or survived.

Article 4

The Silent Jihad

According to Civilus Defendus 'with a hat tip to Kali Politus' at Wordpress.com, there is a standard process of Islamic encroachment to occupy and take over a non-Islamic nation. The article is titled, '4 Stages of Islamic Conquest.' To review the full plan by the Muslim Brotherhood to conquer non-Muslim nations by the process they call 'settlement' review the information at this link. It's from a Muslim Brotherhood plan discovered in 1991, titled, 'An Explanatory Memorandum: On the General Strategic Goal for the Group In North America.'

http://www.discoverthenetworks.org/viewSubCategory.asp?id=1235

Those four stages reported by Wordpress.com and the tactics to enforce or implement those stages are explained:

The first stage is infiltration.

In this stage Muslims begin moving into non-Muslim countries. Their numbers gradually increase at first, and with little or no visible conflicts. Those conflicts that exist are, at first, very subtle. They begin to fit in and ask the host country to be more understanding since they are peaceful, and only victims or where they came from. They continue to claim they are peaceful, although more conflicts between cultures continue to rise. They appeal for more tolerance.

As the size and numbers of more Muslim families increase, they begin to increase in their population and influence; more mosques are built to support those larger populations. Then those mosques become the birthplaces to spread more Islam and to begin exclaiming the stronger Islamic ideologies, and more hatred for the host countries and the historical culture of those host countries.

Once partially established as a part of the community they claim they are being persecuted by 'Islamophobia' and increase their insistence that anyone using Islamophobia against them should be charged with a hate crime. Their further reaction is to threaten legal action against individuals and groups for discrimination and hate crimes. Finally, they propose more interfaith discussions for a better understanding between religions. This is the subterfuge toward more Islamic indoctrination to continue their 'settlement.'

The Wordpress article continues:

"How many nations are suffering from Islamic infiltration? One? A handful? Nearly every nation? The Islamic leadership of the Muslim Brotherhood and others wish to dissolve each nation's sovereignty and replace it with the global imposition of Islamic sharia law. Sharia law, based on the koran, sira and hadith, condemns liberty and forbids equality and is inconsistent with the laws of all Western nations. As the author and historian Serge Trifkovic states:

'The refusal of the Western elite class to protect their nations from jihadist infiltration is the biggest betrayal in history.'"

The second stage is consolidation of power.

This is the phase, the stage where Muslim 'settlers' begin to make their presence more obvious; where they begin to demand more rights, more Islamic freedom, and more acceptance from the local society - although they try to separate themselves through that acceptance. This is as absurd as a Muslim female asking to be free in that Muslim society in which she exists. To stress this point further this is a good time to ask that question:

(If a Muslim female is subjected by Islamic doctrine to be assaulted, maimed, abused, disregarded as a human, and actually killed, in the name of Islam - how can Islam proclaim itself to be 'The religion of Peace?" No other religion, no other country, no other real human being in this world would consider those actions as acts of 'peace.' By its own writings and proclamations, Islamists destroy the foundational basis of their existence. How could terrorizing one person, a female, or a whole nation be considered an act of 'peace?')

That Wordpress article adds this list of accelerated activities by the new Muslim communities:

"Muslim immigrants and host country converts continue demands for accommodation in employment, education, social services, financing and courts."

Even further: Proselytizing increases; Establishment and Recruitment of Jihadi cells begin; There are increased efforts to convert alienated segments of the population to Islam; Muslim leaders revise history to create more Islam into our backgrounds, and they begin to destroy the real evidence that exposes what true Islam really is.

Other subversive and 'settlement' activities include: Increasing negative propaganda against Western history; sweeping up other anti-American groups to give more strength to their operations and tactics against American status-quo. They also begin to infiltrate school systems and other teaching and influencing areas to bring children into their Islamic ideology for continued expansion of their mission. Their settlement strategies and tactics never let up; they continue onward to fulfill that grand design of world Islamism.

They increase their charge to silence their non-Muslims detractors opponents by intimidation and by other charges, such as blasphemy against Islam. They increase their emphasis and growing influence to push for more hate laws against those who oppose their plan and expose their real purpose; which is to make the land they occupy into a purely Muslim nation. According to their own writings and ideologies, they cannot be real Muslims if they stray from this final goal. Activities in this second stage also include the following:

* Efforts to introduce blasphemy and hate laws in order to silence critics.

* Continued focus on enlarging Muslim population by increasing Muslim births and immigration.

* Use of charities to recruit supporters and fund jihad.

* Covert efforts to bring about the destruction of host society from within.

* Development of Muslim political base in non-Muslim host society.

* Islamic Financial networks fund political growth, acquisition of land.

* Highly visible assassination of critics aimed to intimidate opposition.

* Tolerance of non-Muslims diminishes.

* Greater demands to adopt strict Islamic conduct.

* Clandestine amassing of weapons and explosives in hidden locations.

* Overt disregard/rejection of non-Muslim society's legal system, culture.

* Efforts to undermine and destroy power base of non-Muslim religions including and especially Jews and Christians.

Is there a pattern here? Theo van Gogh is murdered in the Netherlands for 'insulting' Islam; the Organization of the Islamic Conference demands 'anti-blasphemy' laws through the United Nations; France is set afire regularly by 'youths' (read Muslims); the rise of (dis-) honor killings...holocaust denial...anti-Semitism...deception re the tenets of Islam; hatred toward Christians and Jews and Hindus and Buddhists. The pattern for all to see is the rise of Islamic intolerance and the covert/cultural jihad to remake host societies into sharia-compliant worlds – to remove host sovereignty and replace it with Islamic sharia law. Sharia law that condemns earthly liberty and individual freedom, that forbids equality among faiths and between the sexes, that rejects the concept of nations outside the global house of Islam, that of dar al-Islam. That Wordpress article continues with an explanation of stage three of the Islamization process.

Stage 3: Open War with Leadership and Culture

35

* Open violence to impose Sharia law and associated cultural restrictions; rejection of host government, subjugation of other religions and customs.

* Intentional efforts to undermine the host government & culture.

* Acts of barbarity to intimidate citizens and foster fear and submission.

* Open and covert efforts to cause economic collapse of the society.

* All opposition is challenged and either eradicated or silenced.

* Mass execution of non-Muslims.

* Widespread ethnic cleansing by Islamic militias.

* Rejection and defiance of host society secular laws or culture.

* Murder of "moderate" Muslim intellectuals who don't support Islamization.

* Destruction of churches, synagogues and other non-Muslim institutions.

* Women are restricted further in accordance with Sharia law.

* Large-scale destruction of population, assassinations, bombings.

* Toppling of government and usurpation of political power.

* Imposition of Sharia law.

The website www.thereligionofpeace.com keeps track of the number of violent jihad attacks as best it can. The site lists more than 14,000 attacks since September 2001. It is worth a visit. What is occurring, however, that is likely inestimable are events where muslims are bullied by other muslims for not being "muslim enough," where non-Muslims are intimidated into doing or not doing what they desire, where remnant populations are in a death spiral simply for being non-muslim in a predominantly muslim area. Christians, Jews, Hindus, Buddhists Animists and Atheists meet with death, property destruction or confiscation, forced conversion, rape, excessive taxation (the jizya), enslavement, riotous mobs and various other forms of islam (in-) justice at the hands of muslims in Sudan, Philippines, Kenya, Malaysia, India, etc. And let us not forget 'death to Apostates' the world over.

Stage 4: Totalitarian Islamic "Theocracy"

Islam becomes the only religious-political-judicial-cultural ideology:

* Sharia becomes the "law of the land.

* All non-Islamic human rights are cancelled.

* Enslavement and genocide of non-Muslim population.

* Freedom of speech and the press eradicated.

* All religions other than Islam are forbidden and destroyed.

* Destruction of all evidence of non-Muslim culture, populations and symbols in country (Buddhas, houses of worship, art, etc).

The House of Islam ("peace"), dar al-Islam, includes those nations that have submitted to Islamic rule, to the soul crushing, liberty-condemning, discriminatory law of Sharia. The rest of the world is in the House of War, dar al-harb, because it does not submit to Sharia, and exists in a state of rebellion or war with the will of 'Allah.' No non-Muslim state or its citizens are "innocent," and remain viable targets of war for not believing in 'Allah.'

The Christian, Jewish, Coptic, Hindu and Zoroastrian peoples of the world have suffered under subjugation for centuries. The Dhimmi-esque are forbidden to construct houses of worship or repair existing ones, economically crippled by the heavy jizya (tax), socially humiliated, legally discriminated against, criminally targeted and generally kept in a permanent state of weakness, fear and vulnerability by Islamic governments.

It should be noted that forced conversions (Egypt) and slavery (Sudan) are still reported. Homosexuals have been hung in the public square in Iran. Young girls are married to old men. Apostates are threatened with death. "Honor" killings are routine. Women are legally second-class citizens, though Muslim males insist they are "treated better" than in the West. These more obvious manifestations may distract from some less obvious ones such as the lack of intellectual inquiry in science, narrow scope of writing, all but non-existent art and music, sexual use and abuse of youth and women, and the disregard for personal fulfillment, joy and wonder. Look into the eyes of a recently married 12 year old girl to see the consequence of the moral deprivation spawned by Islam.

The 4 Stages of Islamic Conquest is also available in pdf format for easy sharing as part of "Liberty vs Sharia"

End of article by Wordpress.com.

Richard Butrick posted an article at Theamericanthinker.com that lists more information about the encroachment of Islam into our lives in America. His article is similar but has a slightly different perspective. His article is titled: The Five Stages of Islam' and covers the same approach to Islam's 'Settlement' process in accordance with their grand strategy outlined by the Muslim Brotherhood. His article begins:

"Forget the Five Pillars of Islam. It is the Five Stages of Islam that threaten the fundamental freedoms of Western Democracy. Freedoms which include freedom of thought, expression, and association and the crucial derived right of freedom of the press. We should never forget that "Islam" means submission -- the opposite of self-determination and Enlightenment values.

Six years ago Dr. Peter Hammond published a remarkable book which included a statistical study of the correlation between Muslim to non-Muslim population ratios and the transition from conciliatory Islam to fascist Islam. The stages are the same in 2011 but the demographics have changed to show an alarming progression. Many European nations and the U.S. are on the cusp of moving to a higher bracket. The demographics change but the story is the same. First comes the taqiyya and the kitman; then comes the Sword of Islam. Imam Rauf, the Ground Zero Mosque promoter, is the current master of taqiyya. He has gulled everyone from Bloomberg to Maureen Dowd of the NYT -- who fanaticizes over male Muslims. Expect doppelgangers of Khomeini for stage 5 and Islamic PEACE at last.

Stage 1. Establish a Beachhead

Population density at 2% (US, Australia, Canada).

Muslims are conciliatory, deferential but request harmless special treatment (foot bath facilities, removal/elimination of that which is offensive to delicate Muslim sensibilities - like walking dogs near Mosques).

Stage 2. Establish Outposts

Population density 2% - 5% (UK, Germany, Denmark).

At 2% to 5%, they begin to proselytize other ethnic minorities and disaffected groups, often with major recruiting from the jails and among street gangs. A recent example is that of Sheikh Abdullah el-Faisal who is back in Jamaica after being kicked out of the UK. Sound harmless? Read on:

The dispatch, dated February 2010, warns that Jamaica could be fertile ground for jihadists because of its underground drug economy, marginalized youth, insufficient security and gang networks in U.S. and British prisons.

Stage 3. Establish Sectional Control of Major Cities.

Population density 5% - 10% (France, Sweden, Netherlands).

First comes the demand for halal food in supermarkets, and the blocking of streets for prayers; then comes the demand for self rule (within their ghettos) under Sharia. When Muslims approach 10% of the population the demands turn to lawlessness. In Paris, we are already seeing car-burnings. Any criticism of Islam results in uprisings and threats, such as in Amsterdam. In France which may be over the 10% range, the minority Muslim populations live in ghettos, within which they are 100% Muslim, and within which they live by Sharia Law. The national police do not even enter these ghettos. There are no national courts, nor schools, nor non-Muslim religious facilities. In such situations, Muslims do not integrate into the community at large. The children attend madrassas. They learn only the Koran. To even associate with an infidel is a crime punishable with death.

Stage 4. Establish Regional Control.

Population density 20% - 50% (Europe 2020?).

After reaching 20%, nations can expect hair-trigger rioting, jihad militia formations, sporadic killings, and the burnings of Christian churches and Jewish synagogues.

Stage 5. Total Control, Brutal Suppression, and Dhimmitude.

Population density > 50%.

Unfettered persecution of non-believers of all other religions (including non-conforming Muslims), sporadic ethnic cleansing (genocide), use of Sharia Law as a weapon, and jizya, the tax placed on infidels. As Muslim population levels increase and all infidels cower in submission there will peace at last. Dar al-Islam is achieved and everyone lives under Sharia and the Koran is the only word.

Our current Western world leaders are suckered by taqiyya and kitman and steering us into stage 3. Allen West seems to get it but I can't see that any of the crop of current GOP contenders really get it. Fear of bigotry at stage 2 is the Islamists' greatest weapon. Crucified on the cross of bigotry -- is that the future of the Western democracies? Bigotry is only bigotry if it is out of touch with reality and it is the suckers who believe the stage 1-2 peace pitch of Islam who are the ones who are out of touch with reality -- not to mention our mesmerized President. The first GOP candidate who announces to Imam Rauf and his supporters, "Fine. A

Mosque at ground zero. But how about a cathedral in Mecca first? It is part of our Christian outreach program of bridge building," will be the first to get it and a big boost in the polls."

The americanthinker.com invites readers at:

www.americanthinker.com/articles/2011/05/the_five_stages_of _islam.html#ixzz3VJb1o5fx. Follow us: @AmericanThinker on Twitter | AmericanThinker on Facebook

Article 5

Islamic No-Go Zones

So, at what stage of Islamic encroachment 'settlement' do we now exist here in America? Is it at stage 1, where Muslims are just beginning to recognize themselves as separate from the rest of America, and are increasing their population to gain more influence? Is it between stages 1 and 2, where they begin to ask for special things in compliance with their religion, such as increasing their demands for halal food, and free times to pray while they are at school and work? Or, is their demands, as indicated above, only at the first minor stage where they ask that dogs not be allowed near their mosques? Perhaps their 'settlement' in America can't be identified as a specific step. Perhaps now it's a combination of all.

Perhaps there's a combination of steps taking place in our nation that are not clearly defined as a step. As most other things in America even the simplest thing or the simplest idea most often becomes a matter of politics - not a matter of definition or certainty. While we watch the front door to determine how far they have encroached, which step, they are slipping in the back door by becoming more influential in politics. For example, Barack Obama has appointed six influential Muslim leaders from the Muslim Brotherhood into his administration. In effect, they are encroaching from the bottom up and from the top down. That's clear; but what about actual physical and armed danger? Are there any indications Muslims are planning for a later stage of 3, 4 or 5? And, could Barack Obama really be involved? First, let's consider "no-go" zones here in America.

This is an article published on Jan 15, 2015 by ETV NEWS. It was reported in a newsletter from Martin Mawyer, Jan. 15, 2015, from the Christian Action Network:

"In the wake of the horrific slaughter at the Charlie Hebdo magazine office in France, the media is suddenly interested in Islamic "no-go" zones scattered throughout Europe where many Muslims are radicalized into jihadists.

(There is some debate about the veracity of this idea, even from high-level leaders of those countries. Most discount the idea that these totally-Muslim enclaves exist in Europe, especially France. They also deny the suggestion that Muslims in these enclaves are radicalized or dangerous.)

But it's important for Americans to understand that right here in the United States we have real "no-go" zones that have been in existence for decades.

On Wednesday I appeared on the Fox and Friends show to discuss America's Islamic no-go zones with host Brian Kilmeade. I explained that a group of Muslims known as Muslims of America (MOA) has as many as two dozen enclaves scattered around the nation, including in Virginia, California, Georgia, South Carolina and New York.

MOA was founded by a Pakistani cleric, Sheikh Mubarik Gilani, and are also known as Jamaat al Fuqra (community of the impoverished).

Several years ago, when my camera crew attempted to enter one of the enclaves in Red House, Virginia, we were angrily and violently forced to leave. Some of the enclaves, including the ones located in Hancock, N.Y., and York, S.C., have entrances protected by armed guards.

The no-go zones that exist right now in America are even more dangerous than the European ones which are so much in the news today. Throughout the al Fuqra camps in the United States, members conduct weapons training and shooting drills. This doesn't happen in the European no-go zones.

And in the U.S. enclaves, they even receive instruction in guerilla combat, how to strangle an enemy and cut a throat. All of these activities have been captured on video.

They exist in remote, rural, often mountainous regions of America where detection is difficult. When they shoot their guns or conduct drills, there is often no one within earshot to hear.

Al Fuqra was once listed on the State Department's watch list of terror organizations – yet today it operates on dozens of enclaves as independent no-go zones with no interference from the outside world. The camps have their own government, with their own mayors and town councils. And because they are Muslim, they use Islamic Sharia law to govern their day-to-day operations.

Polygamy is also practiced on the camps, according to one former resident who spoke with me. He revealed many alarming things about life on the camps, including the fact that the women and elderly are often beaten for disobeying the community rules. These rules can include something as simple as watching TV.

My new film, "Europe's Last Stand: America's Final Warning," took four years to film and produce. During that time I and a camera crew visited dozens of European nations, interviewed hundreds of European officials, experts, clergy and common folks.

I also had an exclusive interview with the radical cleric Anjem Choudary, who has vowed to fly the flag of Islam over the White House. All of these interviews are included in my new documentary, as well as shocking footage of European riots that broke out while we were filming in Great Britain.

In the film, it is clearly demonstrated that Islamists have nearly fulfilled their plan for taking over Europe, and now they have the United States in the crosshairs." End of article.

It's also reported that for several years many aliens from countries other than from Mexico and South America have been infiltrating into the United States across our southern borders - hundreds of them. Some cross directly, but in most cases they cross over after careful planning and preparation. Their normal procedure is to flow into South America, learn the Spanish language then make their crossing. In most cases there is no tracking of them once they cross the border mostly undetected.

In response to long-term speculation that Islamic terrorists were partnering with drug cartels in South America to flow into the United States through our southern borders, I wrote a 350 page novel titled: 'America 20XX: The New World Order.' In the book, I described how terrorists were sneaking across the border as they assisted drug lords deliver their illegal products.

As they assisted with moving drugs, they also delivered and stock-piled weapons in tunnels north of the border; in Arizona. I based that location for the novel from my frequent trips to California, as I drive along Interstate 8 just south of Casa Grande. As I drove along the highway, I would often think what a great location to sneak across the border - it's so isolated. I began my novel's story in that location.

I published 20XX the first week of January, 2011. Two weeks later, news reports revealed a book titled, 'In Memory of our Martyrs' was found on an isolated desert trail just south of Casa Grande. That book was published in Iran and was a compilation of biographical data of many Muslims who had committed suicide bombings. It was found by DHS agents from the Casa Grande office. (More information about that book can be found with an online inquiry, 'Martyrs Book.')

During that same time period many innocents crossing the border with them were found dead - executed. In the novel, these were innocents who learned they were smuggling not only drugs for the drug lords, but also weapons for the terrorists. They were killed to keep them silenced.

Are only Mexicans and South Americans infiltrating across our southern borders? Not according to reported numbers. Recently the Department of Homeland Security had thousands of detainees in its custody who were from Afghanistan, Egypt, Iraq, Iran, Pakistan, Saudi Arabia and Yemen. Statistics reported 108,025 other than Mexican (OTM) were detained in 2006; 165,178 in 2005; and 44,614 in 2004.

Recent reports reveal that OTM apprehensions of illegal aliens increased by 55 percent in 2013. These were mostly from Central and South America, but their original nationality was not reported.

Understanding their modus operandi, an appropriate question might be; how many of them are crossing over as terrorist cell members waiting for the signal to make their terror known?

Another appropriate question complementing that one might be; what happened to all those weapons lost across the border through our government's magnificent 'Fast and Furious' gun operation? Was that operation a random act; or was it part of a more serious and long-term operational plan?

And, pertaining to 'no-go' zones, we must consider the possibility of Islamic terrorists training nearby in South America. Several South American countries such as Venezuela now have closer relationships with Iran than they do with the United States. How close are they ideologically and politically? What long-term danger to they pose to our security?

Article 6

Obama's Religion

When asked about his religion, Obama meekly claims he's a Christian. However, no one knows what he was in his earlier days. Everything more strongly suggests he's a Muslim rather than a real Christian. In researching from his past there seems to be two indications that suggest if he is a Christian, it's just his religion of convenience.

While he was beginning to be more actively involved as a young 'community organizer' he became more involved with churches, primarily Christian churches. His community organizing mentors, on at least one occasion, told him he would be more readily accepted within those church environments if he were a Christian. So, he proclaimed himself to be a Christian. Did he ever actually go to a Christian church? The only church ever mentioned in his past was the one led by Reverend Jeremiah Wright. Wright's church was the Trinity United Church of Christ in Chicago, in which Wright spoke prom the pulpit: "Not God bless America, but God damn America."

This was Obama's church in which he claimed to be a Christian; and he claims he never heard Reverend Wright say or suggest such things as, 'God damn America.' Is that possible? He supported Wright until Wright became a liability to his campaign for president. He threw Wright under the bus the same way he said he would 'never throw his grandmother under the bus.'

From all past indications, he claims to be what is necessary to fit a certain occasion to which he desires to progress. He became a Christian to fulfill two needs. What will he become when it's more expedient and necessary for his future designs, to be a Muslim? He still claims to be a 'Christian.' Does he have a record of being baptized? Clearly, all indications and history strongly suggest he has no religion or he is a Muslim in hiding. It seems his real religion is 'Necessity.'

Why is this question about religion important? Because when he must make a choice about protecting American Christians against Muslim aggression, which side will he choose? At this moment, which religion does he flatter and support most? Let's explore this very important question.

For expediency let's use a convenient list that Joshua Riddle at youngconservatives.com posted on October 2, 2013 about Obama's religious statement regarding Islam. Riddle's article is titled '40 mind-blowing quotes from Barack Obama about Islam and Christianity' but only the first quotes will be shown here. Riddle begins, "This is a great list highlighting how radical President Obama is when it comes to Islam and Christianity:"

#1 "The future must not belong to those who slander the Prophet of Islam."

#2 "The sweetest sound I know is the Muslim call to prayer."

#3 "We will convey our deep appreciation for the Islamic faith, which has done so much over the centuries to shape the world — including in my own country."

#4 "As a student of history, I also know civilization's debt to Islam."

#5 "Islam has a proud tradition of tolerance."

#6 "Islam has always been part of America."

#7 "We will encourage more Americans to study in Muslim communities."

#8 "These rituals remind us of the principles that we hold in common, and Islam's role in advancing justice, progress, tolerance, and the dignity of all human beings."

#9 "America and Islam are not exclusive and need not be in competition. Instead, they overlap, and share common principles of justice and progress, tolerance and the dignity of all human beings."

#10 "I made clear that America is not – and never will be – at war with Islam."

#11 "Islam is not part of the problem in combating violent extremism – it is an important part of promoting peace."

#12 "So I have known Islam on three continents before coming to the region where it was first revealed."

#13 "In ancient times and in our times, Muslim communities have been at the forefront of innovation and education."

#14 "Throughout history, Islam has demonstrated through words and deeds the possibilities of religious tolerance and racial equality."

#15 "Ramadan is a celebration of a faith known for great diversity and racial equality."

#16 "The Holy Koran tells us, 'O mankind! We have created you male and a female; and we have made you into nations and tribes so that you may know one another.'"

#17 "I look forward to hosting an Iftar dinner celebrating Ramadan here at the White House later this week, and wish you a blessed month."

#18 "We've seen those results in generations of Muslim immigrants – farmers and factory workers, helping to lay the railroads and build our cities, the Muslim innovators who helped build some of our highest skyscrapers and who helped unlock the secrets of our universe."

#19 "That experience guides my conviction that partnership between America and Islam must be based on what Islam is, not what it isn't. And I consider it part of my responsibility as president of the United States to fight against negative stereotypes of Islam wherever they appear."

#20 "I also know that Islam has always been a part of America's story."

Now let's examine what Obama says about the Christian religion:

At a fundraiser in San Francisco, in April, 2008, he said, "You go into these small towns in Pennsylvania and, like a lot of small towns in the Midwest, the jobs have been gone now for 25 years and nothing's replaced them. And they fell through the Clinton administration, and the Bush administration, and each successive administration has said that somehow these communities are gonna regenerate and they have not.

And it's not surprising then they get bitter, they cling to guns or religion or antipathy toward people who aren't like them or anti-immigrant sentiment or anti-trade sentiment as a way to explain their frustrations." Should guns and religion be compared in that way? His reference to religion was aiming at Christianity, the dominant religion in those areas. Likely, most Christians would consider these comments and these comparisons as 'blasphemy.'

On September 7, 2008, during an interview with George Stephanopoulos, he referenced, "My Muslim faith." If he is a Muslim, why does he continue to deny it?

When speaking of the Koran, he says, "The Holy Koran." When referencing the Bible, he says, "The Bible." Why does he consider the Koran holy and the Bible not holy?

On June 28, 2006, during his 'Call to Renewal' speech, he mocked three sections of the Bible, including the Sermon on the Mount, which he called 'so radical.' He asked, mockingly, "Can either of these be used to guide public policy?" Both the comments and the comparisons would certainly be considered 'blasphemy' against God and Christianity.

On April 16, 2009, he required the monogram for the name of Jesus be covered before he made his speech at Georgetown University. The monogram above an archway was covered with black painted plywood. Certainly he would not consider this blasphemy - black painted plywood covering the symbol of Jesus. Has he such little respect for Christianity that he would make his blasphemy and his disregard for the religion that conspicuous?

The list of Obama's anti-Christian actions, rhetoric, and blasphemies is too long to identify each individually. A casual review of his actions and comments against churches, especially the Catholic Church, Defense of Marriage Act, cabinet appointments, and exclusion of Christian leaders from religious events are clear proof that he has no respect for God, Christian values, or any reference to the value foundation that allowed the formation of our great country - The United States of America.

And, on September 29, 2009, at a gathering of the Gamaliel Organization, the members prayed to Barack Obama, "Deliver us, Obama." The Book of Revelation reveals that the Antichrist will not be someone 'against' Christ, but who will be acknowledged by his followers to be Christ. Some believe Barack Obama is 'in waiting' to occupy that position. What would give them that idea? Perhaps the Biblical description of that person is a strong clue:

The Antichrist will be a 'man of peace' worshiped by millions, until the 'restrainer' is lifted. Then the real beast will show himself. This lifting of the restrainer most likely is the time when Israel loses its protection from a stronger power, such as the United States. When that restraint is removed Israel will certainly be attacked by an ancient enemy determined to destroy the country and all who live there. That will be the time known as the Abomination of Desolation, when Jews (and Christians) are warned to 'take to the hills.'

The Book of Revelation, 13:5 gives other descriptions, "And there was given unto him a mouth speaking great things and blasphemies." 13:6. "And he opened his mouth in blasphemy against God, to blaspheme his name, and his tabernacle, and them that dwell in heaven." Who do we know, today, who speaks great things, many lies, and blasphemies against God and Christianity. Only one person in a very high position fills these descriptions.

In my search, I have found nothing Obama has said positive about God or the Christian religion. He has never said a negative word about the Muslim religion.

If a conflict were to occur between the two religions, such as a military or terrorist attack against the United States, which side or which religion would he support? Although he took an oath to defend and protect the United States and our Constitution, does anyone believe he really will if he has to make that choice?

Article 7

The Islamic Threat

P rophesy fulfilled before our eyes: The atrocity of 12 more people being slaughtered by Islamic terrorists in France continues to describe a prophesy and reveal the upcoming position of the beast (the Antichrist) in the Book of Revelation. Chapter 17 describes a 'woman' drunken with the blood of the martyrs of Jesus. Another 'woman' was identified in an earlier chapter as a religion - Christianity. Clearly, this woman in Chapter 17 describes another religion as: "And I saw the woman drunken with the blood of the saints, and with the blood of the martyrs of Jesus:" The term 'saints' in Revelation refers to faithful believers, not declared 'Saints.'

This woman, this religion identified in Chapter 17, can be nothing other than the Muslim religion. Many Muslims continue to be 'drunken with the blood of martyrs of Jesus' all over the world, and it gets worse each year; no matter what Barack Obama says or believes. It's those Muslims who are becoming 'drunken with the blood of martyrs of Jesus.'

I just saw an article reporting that 4344 Christians were killed by Islamic radicals for their religion in the year 2014. Approximately 2000 were killed in the year 2013. In 2012 it was only half that number. Unless we take bold action against this Muslim tyranny where will it stop? Will 10,000 Christians be slaughtered this year without serious consequences to those who shield themselves in their religion? Our government, led by Barack Obama, continues to give comfort and support to many of their aims through the Muslim Brotherhood - and political correctness; especially political correctness and other acquiescences that jeopardize our freedom.

We have a president in the White House who continues to support and promote that religion - 'drunken with the blood of martyrs of Jesus.' I wonder what he will be doing in the next few years - if he does not become our nation's first self-appointed president. Will he show his true colors to begin defending the United States of America, as was his oath to become president of the United States? Or, will his support more openly swing in the other direction. Perhaps only time will tell; but what damage might be done in the meantime?

So, what is the greatest Islamic threat to our nation and others? The most brazen threat is already showing itself throughout the Mideast and Africa. The radical Islamists show no mercy, no human decency, or no respect for any mankind as they mercilessly slaughter thousands of innocent people within the lands into which they continue to flow. They 'are drunken with the blood of martyrs of Jesus' as they flow like an amoeba running amuck over every land they touch. According to their dogmatic rhetoric they are the true 'Soldiers of Allah' enforcing his will. Their plan is to make everyone in their wake a Muslim, worshiping Allah and to enforce Sharia law. But, what is this Sharia law they are so desperate to enforce? This list below offered by billionbibles.org summarizes the major parts.

According to the Sharia law:

Theft is punishable by amputation of the right hand.

Criticizing or denying any part of the Quran is punishable by death.

Criticizing or denying Muhammad is a prophet is punishable by death.

Criticizing or denying Allah, the moon god of Islam, is punishable by death.

A Muslim who becomes a non-Muslim is punishable by death.

A non-Muslim who leads a Muslim away from Islam is punishable by death.

A non-Muslim man who marries a Muslim woman is punishable by death.

A man can marry an infant girl and consummate the marriage when she is 9 years old.

Girls' clitoris should be cut (per Muhammad's words in Book 41, Kitab Al-Adab, Hadith 5251).

A woman can have 1 husband, but a man can have up to 4 wives; Muhammad can have more.

A man can unilaterally divorce his wife but a woman needs her husband's consent to divorce.

A man can beat his wife for insubordination.

Testimonies of four male witnesses are required to prove rape against a woman.

A woman who has been raped cannot testify in court against her rapist(s).

A woman's testimony in court, allowed only in property cases, carries half the weight of a man's.

A female heir inherits half of what a male heir inherits.

A woman cannot drive a car, as it leads to fitnah (upheaval).

A woman cannot speak alone to a man who is not her husband or relative.

Meat to be eaten must come from animals that have been sacrificed to Allah - i.e., be Halal.

Muslims should engage in Taqiyya and lie to non-Muslims to advance Islam.

There are more similar stringent rules in Sharia law.

In summary, two things seem very clear from this list from Sharia law. First, it clearly demonstrates a hatred for, and encourages abuse of women, girls, and female babies. There are no restrictions against men that are even comparable to those horrors imposed on females, in that law. One could even imagine a sex lust was involved. That might even be further supported by the concept of a martyr getting 72 virgins at the completion of his or her martyr mission. (Would a female martyr get those same 72 virgins?) What reasonable person could even have conceived of such an idea!

Second, what law process is involved in application of Sharia law? Currently, it seems the determination and application of that law is made by anyone who suspects another of doing something he considers against that law. Who are the 'judge and jury' in this process? Presently in the Mideast and Africa the 'judge and jury' are those who carry guns and knives. Your guilt of a violation is decided by how fast they can put a bullet through your head or behead you. It's that bloodlust described in our Bible. Simply, there are no definitive rules of law in Sharia law. That law is merely an interpretation of the person or group who has the biggest gun or the longest knife.

What is the source of the name; 'Allah?'

In a similar article, Billionbibles.org gives an interesting analysis about Allah, the moon god of Islam, cited above. This is that article:

"Allah Moon God: Is Allah the God of the Bible, or is Allah the moon god of ancient pagan Arabia?

While "Allah" could refer to God literally, the Allah of Islam is the moon god of ancient pagan Arabia. The Arabic word for "god" is "ilah", while "al" is the Arabic for "the". Therefore, "Allah" combines "al" with "ilah" and removes the "i", to literally mean, "the god".

But much like "YHWH/Yahweh/Jehovah" is the personal name of the God of the Bible, "Allah" was also the personal name given to the moon god, the highest of the 360 pagan idols worshipped in Mecca, Muhammad's home town. What evidence is there that Islam's "Allah" is the pagan moon god of ancient Mecca?

Consider what the pagan Arabians did to worship their moon god,

Allah; they prayed while bowing towards K'abah, the "house of Allah" in Mecca that houses a meteorite - a stone from space - several times a day, visited it once a year, and walked around it several times during their visit.

Kabah Hajj: To worship their Allah today:

• Muslims pray bowing towards the K'abah in Mecca five times a day.

• About two million Muslims visit Mecca every year and walk around the K'abah (the black cube, which is 40 feet tall, on the right).

• The Muslim "holy" month of Ramadan starts at the sighting of a new crescent moon.

• Perched atop churches across the world is the cross, the symbol of the sacrifice made by our God. Perched atop mosques across the world is the crescent moon, the symbol of Allah whom Muhammad chose as the god of Islam.

When confronted with the details above, Muslims typically re-assert that "Allah" still means "al" + "ilah" - i.e., "the" + "god" - and is the same as the God of the Bible, not the moon god of pagan Mecca. They even point out that Arabic Christian Bibles use "Allah" to refer to God.

The "Allah" in the current Arabic Christian Bibles is literally "the God" and does refer to the God of the Bible. Advise Muslims that if this is really the "Allah" they are worshipping, then they should stop bowing down toward a meteorite five times a day and the crescent moon should neither start their "holy" month of Ramadan nor top their mosques. If the Allah they are worshipping is the God of the Bible, then they should worship Him as the Bible instructs." End of article.

Clearly, there's a general threat from radical Islam throughout the world. But when considering Islam, the major question becomes 'what is radical Islam?' Is the 'religion of peace' as they refer to themselves, always a religion of peace? Or is there a progression that builds as Islam as a religion of peace takes hold in a region? And, if it is a religion of peace, what happens when that peaceful religion begins enforcing its Sharia law. Does that law suggest peace, or does it suggest terror against females and other who stray from that dogma perceived by those more forceful leaders? Finally, the major question becomes - who decides what is lawful and what is peaceful? Perhaps when speaking of 'peace' we should consider a quote from the Bible:

Daniel 8:25, "And through his policy also he shall cause craft to prosper in his hands; and he shall magnify himself in his heart, and by peace shall destroy many; he shall also stand up against the Prince of princes;"

This concept of 'by peace shall destroy many' is further supported in two other places in the Bible. The first is Daniel 9:27, which reads:

"And he shall enter into a strong and firm covenant with the many for one week. And in the midst of the week he shall cause the sacrifice and offering to cease ; and upon the wing or pinnacle of abominations one who makes desolate, until the full determined end is poured out on the desolator." (Israel will be forced to sign a seven-year covenant of peace. Watch the upcoming news events regarding new covenants and treaties regarding Israel.)

Revelation 13 explains this further. In summary, it says the beast, the antichrist, will have a critical head injury that will make him appear dead. But, he will make a miraculous recovery that will make him appear God-like. Thereafter he will be worshiped by many. (The definition of antichrist is not 'against Christ.' The definition is to appear as Christ.) This will happen halfway through the covenant (The one week in Daniel refers to the seven years in Revelation.) Revelation continues that after that miraculous recovery the 'beast' will show his real power for the last half of that covenant - stated as 42 months (3 1/2 years.) That will begin the 'Abomination of Desolation' in Jerusalem. Jews are encouraged to 'flee to the hills.'

Once again, the Jewish people are threatened with total destruction. The Nazis attempted it the first time, slaughtering without mercy, over six million innocent and unarmed Jews. They didn't have enough time or bullets to kill them all, so to speed the process they used gas as an assembly line process. No one came to their aid. That abomination was discovered after the war ended. Now the new Nazis, the radical Islamists, threaten to finish the task the German Nazis started; to totally annihilate the Jewish people and the Jewish nation.

Will we stand by and watch it happen again? How much support and encouragement will our president, Barack Hussein Obama - the one most influential to offer that protection - offer Israel? Currently, most of his support and encouragement seems to lean toward Israel's avowed enemies - those who plan to wipe them from the face of the earth.

That great battle is briefly introduced and described in the Book of Revelation. It begins in Chapter16:14-21. Chapter 19:11-21 describes the ending of that battle. **God wins.**

If Barack Obama will not offer that support and protection to our only friend and ally in the Middle East, and the nation we consider the foundation of our Christianity, what will he offer to citizens who are here in America - led and grounded by our Christian heritage? Will he and his administration protect us from radical Islamic danger - or must we do that for ourselves?

Article 8

Americans Must be Armed

I began this article with the anticipation of finding valid statistics to support gun ownership by private citizens. In my research, I discovered that many statistics exist, but those statistics are formed based on one's opinion regarding gun ownership. Those who are against the right to own and bear arms present many statistics to prove their point of view. The same for those who promote the right to own and bear arms; they offer statistics to support their point of view. It's for this reason, I decided not to offer any statistics. They could be disproved in either case, by another's opinion based on his or her point of view. Therefore, I will offer other information to encourage every competent American citizen to own a weapon. Our world is becoming too dangerous not to protect yourself - and our freedom. Let's begin by considering some realistic examples:

What would happen if only a few armed terrorists infiltrated across our southern borders and attacked isolated and unarmed citizens? Would their purpose be to conquer the United States by military force? No; their purpose would be to create a pattern of fear that would curtail many of our freedoms and expectations of life as free citizens. What would the gun-haters likely do if that were to happen. Of course, they would suggest we need more police or military protection along the borders. Obviously their concern is that guns don't get into the hands of American citizens to protect themselves. They consider those Americans dangerous and irresponsible, unworthy of their own defense of life.

What would happen to unarmed citizens if only two or three Islamic terrorists blocked a major highway on a long stretch with no exits, and began walking along that highway shooting or beheading every person in those automobile? If citizens were not armed, that slaughter could continue until enough armed police arrived. How long would that take? Imagine the fear and horror of those defenseless people.

What would the gun-haters say then? Perhaps they would say or suggest those private citizens should not have been on the highway, anyway, at that time. Perhaps they are the same people who would claim the drivers were polluting the atmosphere with their gasoline emissions. Seriously, would they express more concern about gun-ownership than about those people's lives and the fear and horror they experienced? Some gun-haters are such total zealots I'm not sure what they might say.

Perhaps those zealots might change their minds if those highway blockades became so numerous that it affected the flow of economic transportation; the flow of food and other goods and services. Would they complain about the lack of produce on store shelves - or would they be more concerned that someone might accidently shoot themselves if they had a personal weapon strapped to their side? Or, might they suggest that every produce transport truck must have an armed police office in the cab to accompany the driver?

Perhaps when those gun-haters got hungry or thirsty, or personally looked down the barrel of a gun pointing at them, they might have a different point of view. They might develop that point of view our ancestors faced when they were fighting for our freedom during the formation of our great nation. Or, would they have opposed private gun ownership at that time. When will 'too late' be too late for them to change their point of view?

So, as an ordinary citizen what should we do? We must arm ourselves - and let the terrorists and other evil throughout the world know that every citizen is armed and ready to use our weapons against them. If and when you are attacked, calling 911 might be too late to protect you and your family. It wouldn't take that long for a Muslim terrorist to either shoot you and your family with an AK-47, or cut your head off with a big knife. Being armed and letting the world know you are well armed will likely prevent that attack altogether.

Obama and his administration, as well as many other gun-haters, are against the arming of private citizens. Most certainly, every gun being purchased and every ammunition sale is now recorded at the NSA center in Bluffdale, Utah. Plus, in many cases the sale of ammunition is already being allocated. This new NSA center in Bluffdale, Utah has the capability to monitor everything every citizen on EARTH does, buys or says for the next 20 years. Rest assured, anyone who buys any gun or gun-related item will be recorded as a gun owner. If and when the tyranny begins, that person will get a knock on their door; and probably in the middle of the night. Most people are at home in the middle of the night.

(Be aware if you plan to buy a firearm that the availability of ammunition must be considered first. Don't buy a firearm if you can't buy a sufficient quantity of bullets at the same time. Ammunition will be the first item confiscated. For example, one of the most popular target pistols and small-game hunting rifles fires a .22 LR, long rifle, bullet. Presently, many stores **do not** have them stocked. Why will ammunition be controlled first? Because many families own weapons handed down from generation to generation that have no record of ownership – unless those families have recently bought ammunition for those weapons. Another consideration: Why have representatives from Google been working so closely with the Obama administration lately? Draw your own conclusions. My thought is that it must be in some way related to that NSA Center hub in Bluffdale, Utah.)

If and when terrorist attacks occur, what will likely be Obama's first reaction? To stop the sale of private weapons and ammunition, and confiscate those from gun owners to 'prevent the spread of terrorism.' From an act of desperation - and one might suspect cooperation with a greater goal of the Muslim Brotherhood - those patriots trying to defend America and freedom might be the very ones listed as 'terrorists' by our government.

Homeland Security has already suggested veterans returning from wars are vulnerable to being coaxed into becoming domestic terrorists. Also, many in our government have labeled Tea Party members as 'anarchists' and 'terrorists.' If we are attacked by real Islamic terrorists would Barack Obama and his administration take action against these two groups by suggesting they were part of the actual terrorists. At minimum, they certainly would not be allowed to own weapons or ammunition to defend themselves.

Now, this is the pertinent and life-saving question - and the reason every competent U.S. citizen must be armed. Would terrorists even attempt such an action if they knew or suspected most of those people in the automobiles were armed and prepared to shoot them? I think not. It would defeat their plan and purpose to create terror.

In this dangerous world threatened by ungodly Islamic terrorists - and others, we must be armed. Our government must not be allowed to prevent us from getting our weapons of defense - and they must not be allowed to confiscate them under any pretenses - none whatsoever under any circumstances.

One of those pretenses is the claim that many 'anarchist citizens' are hoarding guns and ammunition to defend themselves against a tyrannical government. They consider the 'preppers' part of those anarchists. In reality, even the preppers know they could not defend themselves against our government forces. That is totally out of the question and an unreasonable consideration.

The preppers are positioning to defend themselves and their families against two aggressive possibilities. One is against radical Islamic terrorists who might invade their area. The other threat they try to guard against are the roving bands of marauders who might be reactionary to an oppressive government's actions against common citizens. These marauders would be seeking food and other survival items if and when disenfranchised by the government. Preppers' actions are purely to defend and protect themselves and their families - not to participate in revolution against the government. But - this will be the logical excuse the government will employ when they try to confiscate those weapons.

What can we common citizens do, at this time, to protect ourselves and America? The most urgent action we must take is to make every candidate running in any upcoming election declare, without equivocation or evasion, if they support the unimpeded right for every American to own a personal defensive weapon. Those who say, or suggest 'NO' should be voted out of office or never be allowed to enter an office responsible for our safety and security - period.

And, you must arm yourself as an American patriot. The evil world must know we are Americans and we are prepared to defeat their evil - without any hesitation whatsoever. We must and will stand armed and united to defend our free nation against all enemies, 'foreign and domestic.'

More information about the NSA center can be found at this link:

http://www.theblaze.com/stories/2013/07/01/seven-stats-to-know-about-nsas-utah-data-center-as-it-nears-completion/

Conclusion

In consideration of all the information offered above perhaps it's important to have answers to three questions. The first question is: how dedicated is the United States to Israel's protection? The second is: what role will our military play if a president were to show his tyrannical stripes and order them to attack or subdue a nation he would proclaim as threatening to the United States government. The third question is: what kind of snake must we protect ourselves against?

Will the United States Protect Israel?

In the 1930s and 1940s the world stood by and watched as German Nazis began to wreak havoc on Jews scattered throughout Europe. Eventually, they rounded up Jews and herded them as animals through a slaughter house as they killed over six million of them without any thought of mercy or humanity. The real atrocity wasn't discovered until after Germany surrendered. At that time, the whole world agreed with the Jewish people to proclaim, 'Never again.'

Now, Israel depends largely on the United States to provide shelter and security to their existence; as a nation and as human beings. Until recently that commitment to Israel and its people was unquestioned. Israel's enemies knew that to commit a major attack on Israel was the same as committing an attack against the United States. Now the understanding of that commitment doesn't exist.

Now, Barack Obama snubs his nose at Israel as he compliments its neighbors with great praise of their contributions throughout history.

He has made it well known by his indirect words and actions that he will no longer stand by Israel in Israel's greatest hour of need. Obama has already proved himself a liar and deceiver of biblical proportions. There's no doubt that his claim to be a Christian is his greatest deception. Now Israel understands who their greatest protector is; and it's not the president of the United States.

Will Our Military Fire on U.S. Citizens?

During the great transition of the Soviet Union, Boris Yeltzin stood before tank cannon pointed directly at his face - and he didn't back down. Instead of protecting the status quo of the Soviet Union, the Russian soldiers climbed out of their tanks and rushed to embrace and support Yeltzin. If that similar situation were to occur in the United States, would American military personnel fire on their fellow citizens whom they know are trying to protect the U.S. Constitution? Is that why Barack Obama has fired and continues to fire many senior U.S. generals in the military. Are they being screened and selected to insure only those left in the military will support him regardless of his actions and decisions?

If that were the case it would be nothing new. Vladimir Lenin and Joseph Stalin did that to their generals in Russia before the formation of the Soviet Union. Stalin so depleted his army of professional leaders that when they were attacked by Germany, Russia was almost destroyed. The only thing that saved them was the weather. Many German soldiers froze to death on the battle field and their weapons became inoperative; while they were only a few miles outside Moscow.

Armed Patriots   Will Clark

Perhaps we will not know the answer to this question until that dangerous situation were to occur. Hopefully, every military person will already have considered what he or she would do if presented with that difficult dilemma.

What Snakes do we Face?

Many who have no experience with snakes probably imagine a snake is just a snake. Some are poisonous and some are not; some are long and some are short. An inexperienced person would never know the difference. But, snakes are different and have different personalities, if one chooses to call it 'personality.'

Some are quiet and sneaky; while others are more aggressive and ready to attack. I'll use two real incidents from my past for examples. First, I'll describe the personality of a copperhead snake.

When I was about twelve years old I went fishing with my uncle as we often did. Our path to the fishing pond took us through a large sage patch that ended abruptly adjoining a large pine tree area. The walk was about two miles. We walked in those days because not everyone had an automobile. The walk there was uneventful. But on the way back, I had a surprise experience.

My uncle was walking about ten feet ahead just before we exited the large area of pine trees to enter the sage patch. Suddenly from my peripheral vision I saw a stick, or what I thought was a stick, flip toward my legs after he had stepped in that area. By reflex, I immediately lurched backward to keep the stick from hitting me. I never looked to see what it was but my uncle turned and told me to move out of the way. He killed the snake with a limb while I just watched trying to understand why I wasn't more careful. I was experienced enough in the woods to know to watch for snakes.

75

Had my reflexes not forced me to jump back, that snake would certainly have bit my leg. We were out in a primitive area, and it would have taken nearly an hour to get anywhere for help. As a kid, it was just another event; another part of country life. Today, I count my blessings.

My next close event with a snake was with a cottonmouth, often called a 'water mocassin.' Of course I had seen many and had cautiously played with them, with a stick at a distance, but I had never had this happen to me before. Knowing they preferred to stay in or near water areas, when I was about sixteen, I often watched for them to stick their heads up from the water in our small pond, and would shoot them with my shotgun.

One August afternoon, often called the 'dog days of summer' in the south because ordinarily it's so hot, and there's never a cool breeze, I stood on the levee watching for the next head to pop up. It was hot and still, without any breeze to temper the heat. Ordinarily, birds were flying around and chirping near the water, but on this afternoon everything was quiet as I watched the calm surface. Suddenly I heard a small noise near my feet. I didn't move because I didn't want to alert any snake that might pop his head to the top. I imagined that small noise was probably a grasshopper moving to a different position. It was that quiet.

When I heard that almost silent noise again, I slowly moved my head to glance down at that location. It wasn't a grasshopper; it was a cottonmouth, about three feet long, coiled in the striking position. For those who don't know, the striking position is an S shape with the head leaning backward over the first coil. The snake's color and triangular shaped head instantly told me it was a poisonous cottonmouth. He was silently waiting and probably wondering what he should do - as was I. Understanding snakes as I did, I knew if I made a quick movement to jump he would probably strike before I could get clear. His head was only twelve inches from my feet; and I was barefoot, as most southern farm lads are in the summertime. I was concerned, but I didn't panic.

Of course, I stared at his head as I slowly moved my upper body to put my shotgun in position to point at his head and pull the trigger. He didn't move, and my lower body, particularly my legs, didn't move. This was an old-fashioned shotgun with a hammer that had to be cocked to fire. When I had it pointed into what I thought was the right position, I cocked the hammer and pulled the trigger. Fortunately for me, not the snake, I didn't miss. The shotgun blast threw the snake about ten feet from me. I didn't have to check his pulse to know he was dead. That was the last time I stood quietly staring at the pond's surface on a dog-day afternoon.

Over the past few years I've had two other minor experiences with copperheads, which proved to me their 'personality' is standard. Once I toyed with a very young one, about eight inches long. When I placed a long stick near his head he would jump up about half the length of his body to strike at the end of the stick. He showed an extremely aggressive attitude that never waned. Another time while I was on a golf course cart path I came upon a large copperhead warming himself on the cart path in the early morning sun. Obviously, he didn't want to leave because he raised his body to half-length and made a threatening gesture before he finally relinquished his warm spot and slithered away, stopping twice to raise his head and look back at me. I was 75 at that time, and was very thankful I was in a golf cart. It was faster than my current running speed.

Now, at this time, you might wonder why stories about different snakes are important to the purpose of this book. I included these stories, true stories, to demonstrate that we must know our enemy. As snakes have different personalities and characteristics so do our current-day enemies; those who threaten to kill - to destroy - our American way of life. A snake is not just a snake. Some are out front - in your face; others are sneaky and subtle to accomplish the same purpose. That purpose is to kill you.

First are the copperheads. These are the Islamic terrorists who vow to kill us and everyone who doesn't comply with their ungodly wishes and demands. They fearlessly attack those most vulnerable without mercy or without remorse. Their purpose is to intimidate you, dominate you, and then kill you. They are blindly driven to accomplish an ungodly mission in some godly name that they themselves don't even understand. That 'cause' is simply a justification to fulfill a kill lust.

The only way to stop this copperhead's aggression is to kill it. And, if that's not the appropriate resolution at the time, that snake must know you have enough big shotguns aimed at his head that he will not invade your territory. He must know he will be dead, and he will not have free range to slaughter innocent people at will. He must pay a heavy price for even making the attempt.

Simply, if those copperheads know every American citizen has a big gun aimed at their individual and personal heads, they will seek their blood-lust elsewhere. Soon their safe sanctuaries will be depleted - if more people show the same resolve to defeat them - to kill them without hesitation. They are vicious and unrelenting copperheads.

So, what about those calmer and more subtle cottonmouths? The Muslim Brotherhood is another snake attacking America and other Western democracies. The Muslim Brotherhood is the cottonmouth of the snake world. It accomplishes its purpose by being sneaky and subtle, by easing into vulnerable places to increase its influence and power in a vulnerable and accepting nation. You don't recognize the danger until you look down and see that serpent coiled at your feet ready to strike; ready to strike a blow that will kill all the dreams our forefathers planned and sacrificed so much for our future. Yes, that cottonmouth is very patient, and no matter how long it takes will join the copperhead to accomplish its deadly mission. That mission is to eliminate all infidels from the face of the earth. In the end, the cottonmouth and the copperhead are equally dangerous. Their final purpose is to kill you.

The Book of Revelation in the Bible makes two very important and connected points to give a clue about what's happening in our world today. In Chapters 2 and 3, John writes letters to the seven churches in Asia, as dictated to him by the Spirit. All seven churches were given this same admonition: "He that hath and ear, let him hear what the Spirit saith unto the churches." The letters are admonitions and warning of things to come.

In Chapter 17, He gives one specific warning. After having described a 'woman' as a religion in Chapter 12, he describes another 'woman,' religion, in Chapter 17: "And I saw the woman drunken with the blood of the saints, and with the blood of the martyrs of Jesus." After having read the Books of Daniel and Revelation many, many times, I have no doubt this means Muslims, that religion, will be drunken with the blood of Christians they will continue to slaughter until the end of that 'great battle.' Could there be any other interpretation of the meaning of these writings? Do we not see news reports everyday of that happening across our world? These snakes will not change their personality; it's instinctive; it's in there genes. They simply have a blood lust that must be stopped.

Now, here comes the very deeply religious question: If God had not wanted us to do something about this tyranny, against

Christians and humanity, from the other 'woman' would He have warned us about that horror? He said, 'those who have an ear' do something! He didn't say He would take care of the problem by Himself. Certainly, He is the Almighty, but we must realize that we are His hands. Our hands are one of those 'two-edged swords' coming from His mouth to defeat that evil. Will we use those hands to do His will, or will we continue to ignore His warnings to those 'who have an ear?'

The gun-haters will continue to deny the danger. They fear guns more than the purpose for people to have guns. They 'don't have an ear.' They are trying to force us to walk barefoot through tall, snake-infested grass.

Reject their ill-advised and ungodly efforts and pursuits. Own a weapon and ammunition, know how to use it; and we must let the whole world know we will defend our nation and our freedom. Be an armed patriot - and be proud of it. Eventually, the gun-haters will be embarrassed and will thank you for being an armed patriot.

# # #

About the Author

Will Clark's author experiences began by writing inspection and evaluation reports in the U.S. Air Force. He is a retired Air Force officer and a Vietnam veteran, serving in Saigon from 1966 to 1967. His other overseas assignments include Misawa, Japan and Ankara, Turkey.

In 1995, he authored a book, *How to Learn*, as a county-wide study skills project to encourage students to improve their grades in DeSoto County, Mississippi. Education supporters printed and distributed four thousand copies. He also wrote a weekly education column for a local newspaper, *The Desoto County Tribune,* the following school year.

His next published book was *School Bells and Broken Tales*, a parody of nursery rhyme characters, also a motivation and education book for children. His other books include *Shades of Retribution*, a historical novel, and *Simply Success*, a motivation guide for students and employees.

His action novels include a trilogy based on Atlantis and crystals. The first book is titled: *The Atlantis Crystal*. The second book is titled: *She Waits In Atlantis*. The third is: *Return to Atlantis*. This trilogy is based on his travels while assigned to Turkey, site of the ancient city of Troy.

His previous political action novel, *666: Mark of the Beast*, is a sequel to another political action novel, *America 20XX: The New World Order*.

Clark and his wife, Marie, live in Diamondhead, Mississippi, where they play golf with many friends.

For more information about the author visit:

http://www.authorsden.com/visit/author.asp?authorid=1496

Things We Must Never Forget
Until We Know All the Answers

Benghazi

Why were four Americans killed?
Where was Hillary Clinton while it was happening?
Where was Barack Obama while it was happening?
Why did they lie and blame the event on a video?
Why were rescuers on 'stand by' told to 'stand down?'

Fast and Furious

Who authorized the operation?
Why did the operation continue after weapons were lost?
Why did the procedure have no procedure?
Why weren't tracking devices used?

The IRS Scandal

What was the highest level involved?
Who initiated it?
Why hasn't anyone been fired or reprimanded?
What dangers could be unleashed by this organization?

Greatest Quotes
of
Our Time

Michelle Obama
February 18, 2008
"For the first time in my adult life I am proud of my country."
(Age 44)

Barack Obama
March 9, 2008
"We are no longer a Christian nation - at least not just."

September 25, 2012
Remarks to the UN General Assembly
"The future must not belong to those who slander Islam."

Nancy Pelosi
March 9, 2010
"We have to pass the bill so that you can find out what is in it."

Hillary Clinton
January 23, 2013
"What difference, at this point, does it make?"

December 3, 2014
"...showing respect even for one's enemies, trying to understand
and insofar as psychologically possible, empathize with their
perspective and point of view."

Other Books by the Author

Novels:
Shades of Retribution
The Atlantis Crystal
She Waits in Atlantis
Return to Atlantis
America 20XX: The New World Order
666: Mark of the Beast
Death Drones: 2025

Children's Books:
Forest Trails and Fairy Tales
Wishing Wells and Broken Tales
Student Study Skills
American Heroes: Students Who Learn

Non-Fiction:
Simply Success
The Education Jungle
How to Learn
The Day America Died
Obama's Ring: The Seat of Satan
Managing Without Conflict
The Peer Pressure Monster
The War on Christians
Who is the Antichrist
The War on Christians
The Seven Spirits
Obama, Hillary, Saul Alinsky and their Useful Idiots

www.ingramcontent.com/pod-product-compliance
Lightning Source LLC
Chambersburg PA
CBHW070556290526
45790CB00002B/710